CW01467368

# MongoDB Essentials

A quick introduction

The MongoDB Team

**‹packt›**

# MongoDB Essentials

Copyright © 2025 Packt Publishing

*All rights reserved*. No part of this book may be reproduced, stored in a retrieval system, or transmitted in any form or by any means, without the prior written permission of the publisher, except in the case of brief quotations embedded in critical articles or reviews.

Every effort has been made in the preparation of this book to ensure the accuracy of the information presented. However, the information contained in this book is sold without warranty, either express or implied. Neither the authors, nor Packt Publishing or its dealers and distributors, will be held liable for any damages caused or alleged to have been caused directly or indirectly by this book.

Packt Publishing has endeavored to provide trademark information about all of the companies and products mentioned in this book by the appropriate use of capitals. However, Packt Publishing cannot guarantee the accuracy of this information.

**Portfolio Director**: Sunith Shetty
**Relationship Lead**: Sathya Mohan
**Project Managers**: Aniket Shetty & Sathya Mohan
**Content Engineer**: Siddhant Jain
**Technical Editor**: Aniket Shetty
**Copy Editor**: Safis Editing
**Indexer**: Tejal Soni
**Proofreader**: Siddhant Jain
**Production Designer**: Deepak Chavan

First published: September 2025

Production reference: 1220825

Published by Packt Publishing Ltd.
Grosvenor House
11 St Paul's Square
Birmingham
B3 1RB, UK.

ISBN 978-1-80670-609-9
www.packtpub.com

*To the MongoDB community—builders, architects, operators, and learners—*
*whose curiosity, feedback, and passion continue to shape the evolution of MongoDB.*

# Foreword

MongoDB wasn't built to follow trends or repackage legacy paradigms. It was designed to fundamentally rethink how data should be handled in modern applications, where systems scale globally, evolve rapidly, and process a mixture of structured, semi-structured, and unstructured data.

This book captures over a decade of real-world lessons, patterns, and innovations in a practical, quick-start guide. Authored by the team at MongoDB that enables developers and technologists, this book is not just about using MongoDB; it's about understanding how and why it works.

Inside, you'll explore core topics such as the document model, indexing strategies, and the aggregation framework, as well as modern capabilities such as full-text search, vector search, and retrieval-augmented generation. Each chapter is designed to help you develop an intuitive understanding and not just memorize syntax.

Whether you're new to MongoDB or looking to sharpen your architectural and performance thinking, this guide is designed to get you productive—fast.

We hope it sparks not just solutions but new ideas.

*The MongoDB Team*

# Foreword

MongoDB wasn't built to follow trends or repackage legacy paradigms. It was designed to fundamentally rethink how data should be handled in modern applications, where systems scale globally, evolve rapidly, and process a mixture of structured, semi-structured, and unstructured data.

This book captures over a decade of real-world lessons, patterns, and innovations in a practical, quick-start guide. Authored by the team at MongoDB that enables developers and technologists, this book is not just about using MongoDB; it's about understanding how and why it works.

Inside, you'll explore core topics such as the document model, indexing strategies, and the aggregation framework, as well as modern capabilities such as full-text search, vector search, and retrieval-augmented generation. Each chapter is designed to help you develop an intuitive understanding and not just memorize syntax.

Whether you're new to MongoDB or looking to sharpen your architectural and performance thinking, this guide is designed to get you productive—fast.

We hope it sparks not just solutions but new ideas.

*The MongoDB Team*

# Contributors

This book was written and reviewed by the team behind MongoDB University—a diverse group of engineers, educators, and subject matter experts committed to helping you succeed with MongoDB.

# MongoDB Skill Badges

After reading this book, you can validate and showcase your knowledge with official **MongoDB Skill Badges**, which are short, hands-on credentials you can earn in just 60–90 minutes. These are free, practical, and available on `learn.mongodb.com`.

**Topics include the following:**

| MongoDB Skill | |
|---|---|
| Relational to Document Model | Schema Patterns and Anti-patterns |
| Advanced Schema Patterns and Anti-patterns | Schema Design Optimization |
| CRUD Operations | Query Optimization |

| MongoDB Skill | MongoDB Skill |
|---|---|
| Indexing Design Fundamentals | Fundamentals of Data Transformation |
| Vector Search Fundamentals | RAG with MongoDB |
| AI Agents with MongoDB | Sharding Strategies |
| Monitoring Tooling | Performance Tools & Techniques |

These badges offer a pathway for continuous learning, whether you're building applications, designing schemas, optimizing queries, or exploring advanced use cases like AI and distributed systems.

MongoDB Skill — Indexing Design Fundamentals

MongoDB Skill — Fundamentals of Data Transformation

MongoDB Skill — Vector Search Fundamentals

MongoDB Skill — RAG with MongoDB

MongoDB Skill — AI Agents with MongoDB

MongoDB Skill — Sharding Strategies

MongoDB Skill — Monitoring Tooling

MongoDB Skill — Performance Tools & Techniques

These badges offer a pathway for continuous learning, whether you're building applications, designing schemas, optimizing queries, or exploring advanced use cases like AI and distributed systems.

# Table of Contents

# Preface

Before you get started, you may be asking yourself: *"What makes MongoDB different?"*

To put it simply, MongoDB wasn't built to follow trends or repackage old ideas. MongoDB reimagines how data should be handled in modern software, where systems evolve rapidly, operate globally, and work with structured and unstructured information side by side.

This book is a quick start for anyone who needs to get up and running with MongoDB. Whether you're building software, managing systems, or evaluating how MongoDB fits into your stack, this book covers the fundamentals step by step. We'll look at how MongoDB organizes data, runs queries, scales out, and integrates into modern workflows.

Each chapter builds your understanding of how MongoDB works by focusing on not just the mechanics, but the reasoning behind the design. You'll learn how to think in terms of documents, model using access patterns, and apply design patterns that work from development to production.

Whether you're just starting out or sharpening your understanding, this book will give you the clarity and confidence to use MongoDB effectively.

## How this book will help you

This book is designed to act as a quick-start guide if you're new to MongoDB or need a refresher. It introduces key concepts through real-world examples, including data modeling principles, CRUD operations, the aggregation pipeline, and performance tips. This book also includes steps for setting up MongoDB, reducing friction, and giving you hands-on experience from the beginning of your journey.

## Who this book is for

This book is for anyone interested in using MongoDB, including developers, database administrators, system architects, students, managers, and decision-makers who want to familiarize themselves with what a modern database can offer. Whether you're building your first application or exploring what MongoDB can offer you, this book serves as your first step on your MongoDB journey.

# What this book covers

*Chapter 1, MongoDB Architecture*, explores the building blocks of MongoDB's distributed design and familiarizes you with the document model, replica sets, and sharding.

*Chapter 2, Getting Started with MongoDB*, covers how to install the required tools, create a local deployment, and your first database and collection.

*Chapter 3, Data Modeling*, covers the fundamentals of schema design and data modeling in MongoDB.

*Chapter 4, CRUD Operations*, shows you how to interact with your data.

*Chapter 5, Aggregation*, shows you how to use the aggregation framework to perform complex data analysis efficiently.

*Chapter 6, Performance Strategies and Tools*, explains the tools available to ensure that your queries run fast and scale well.

*Chapter 7, Intelligent Applications with MongoDB*, covers the MongoDB tools that support the development of AI-based applications: Atlas Search and Atlas Vector Search.

# To get the most out of this book

You will require the following software:

| Software covered in the book | Operating system requirements |
|---|---|
| MongoDB version 4.4 or newer | Windows, macOS, or Linux |
| MongoDB Shell (monogsh) | Windows, macOS, or Linux |

After reading this book, we encourage you to check out some of the other resources available at https://learn.mongodb.com/.

## Download the color images

We also provide a PDF file that has color images of the screenshots/diagrams used in this book. You can download it here: https://packt.link/gbp/9781806706099.

## Conventions used

There are a number of text conventions used throughout this book.

`CodeInText`: Indicates code words in text, database table names, folder names, filenames, file extensions, pathnames, dummy URLs, user input, and X/Twitter handles. For example: "To insert a new book into the `books` collection, you use the `insertOne` command."

A block of code is set as follows:

```
{
    "title": "Designing APIs with MongoDB",
    "author": "Alex Smith",
    "genres": ["Technology", "Databases"],
    "inStock": true,
    "publisher": {
        "name": "MongoDB Press",
        "location": "New York"
    }
}
```

Any command-line input or output is written as follows:

```
brew install mongodb-atlas-cli
brew install mongosh
brew install mongodb-compass  # Optional GUI
```

**Bold**: Indicates a new term, an important word, or words that you see on the screen. For instance, words in menus or dialog boxes appear in the text like this. For example: "**Sharding** is MongoDB's approach to horizontal scaling."

> Warnings or important notes appear like this.

> Tips and tricks appear like this.

# Get in touch

Feedback from our readers is always welcome.

**General feedback**: If you have questions about any aspect of this book or have any general feedback, please email us at customercare@packt.com and mention the book's title in the subject of your message.

**Errata**: Although we have taken every care to ensure the accuracy of our content, mistakes do happen. If you have found a mistake in this book, we would be grateful if you could report this to us. Please visit http://www.packt.com/submit-errata, click **Submit Errata**, and fill in the form.

**Piracy**: If you come across any illegal copies of our works in any form on the internet, we would be grateful if you would provide us with the location address or website name. Please contact us at copyright@packt.com with a link to the material.

**If you are interested in becoming an author**: If there is a topic that you have expertise in and you are interested in either writing or contributing to a book, please visit http://authors.packt.com/.

## Share your thoughts

Once you've read *MongoDB Essentials*, we'd love to hear your thoughts! Scan the QR code below to go straight to the Amazon review page for this book and share your feedback.

https://packt.link/r/1806706091

Your review is important to us and the tech community and will help us make sure we're delivering excellent quality content.

# Download a free PDF copy of this book

Thanks for purchasing this book!

Do you like to read on the go but are unable to carry your print books everywhere?

Is your eBook purchase not compatible with the device of your choice?

Don't worry, now with every Packt book you get a DRM-free PDF version of that book at no cost.

Read anywhere, any place, on any device. Search, copy, and paste code from your favorite technical books directly into your application.

The perks don't stop there, you can get exclusive access to discounts, newsletters, and great free content in your inbox daily.

Follow these simple steps to get the benefits:

1. Scan the QR code or visit the link below:

https://packt.link/free-ebook/9781806706099

2. Submit your proof of purchase.
3. That's it! We'll send your free PDF and other benefits to your email directly.

# 1

# Mongodb Architecture

To use MongoDB effectively, it helps to first understand how it works under the hood. This chapter introduces the core components that make MongoDB a flexible, powerful, and developer-friendly database. Whether you're building a small app or scaling a large distributed system, the concepts covered here will form the foundation of your understanding.

This chapter will cover the following topics:

- How MongoDB stores and organizes data using documents instead of rows
- How MongoDB stores documents in collections instead of tables
- The importance of indexes to support fast, efficient queries
- MongoDB's storage engine and query execution architecture
- MongoDB's JSON-based query language
- The distributed design on MongoDB, including replica sets and sharding
- An overview of client libraries and drivers for interacting with the database

By the end of this chapter, you'll have a solid grasp of MongoDB's core building blocks and be better equipped to make informed decisions about how to design and interact with your data.

## Building blocks of MongoDB

Before we dive into queries, documents, or code, it's worth taking a moment to step back and ask a bigger question: "*What is MongoDB?*"

If you've worked with relational database management systems (RDBMSs), many of the core ideas will feel familiar, such as rows, tables, and columns. But in MongoDB, these go by different names: documents, collections, and fields. However, MongoDB doesn't just rename the parts, it redefines how data is stored and accessed, based on how modern applications operate. MongoDB emphasizes flexibility, scalability, and developer experience.

At its core, MongoDB offers a flexible alternative to traditional relational databases, while standing apart from other types of NoSQL systems. Key-value databases are often praised for their speed and simplicity, while relational databases offer powerful querying and transactional integrity. MongoDB brings the best of both: you get performance and a flexible schema with the querying depth and indexing power of traditional RDBMSs. This isn't just about convenience, but architectural alignment with how developers build applications today.

## Documents, not rows

Let's start with the most important concept for understanding MongoDB: **documents**.

In MongoDB, data lives in JSON-like structures called documents, which are stored internally in a format known as **Binary JSON** (**BSON**). Documents are self-contained units of information, often representing a single object or entity in your app. You can think of documents as rows in a table, but with nested fields, arrays, and varying structures.

Here's a simple example of a document representing a book in a bookstore catalog:

```
{
    "title": "Designing APIs with MongoDB",
    "author": "Alex Smith",
    "genres": ["Technology", "Databases"],
    "inStock": true,
    "publisher": {
        "name": "MongoDB Press",
        "location": "New York"
    }
}
```

This isn't a collection of references to other tables. It's the entire book, with everything you need to render it in your app, all in one place.

## Collections and indexes

In MongoDB, a **collection** is the next organizational structure after documents. Collections group related documents, much like a table in a relational database, but with an optional schema. You're free to store documents of similar shapes in the same collection, which means MongoDB is ideal for evolving data structures. Collections live inside databases, which provide logical separation. A single MongoDB deployment can contain multiple databases, each isolated from the other.

While collections organize related documents, **indexes** optimize how efficiently MongoDB can retrieve those documents.

MongoDB supports powerful indexing capabilities, including the following:

- A default `_id` index on every collection
- Support for indexing any field, including nested fields and array values
- A specialized B-tree-like structure for storing indexes, enabling fast lookups and efficient range queries, similar to relational systems

Behind the scenes, MongoDB's ability to put indexes to work relies on the underlying architecture of the mongod process, which includes a sophisticated query engine and a high-performance storage engine. In the next section, we'll take a look at those components.

## Storage engine and query execution

Every MongoDB deployment is powered by a mongod process, the core server that stores your data, handles queries, and keeps the whole system running smoothly. Whether it's running on your laptop or in a distributed production cluster, every mongod instance includes three critical architectural layers: the query planner, the execution engine, and the storage engine.

Let's say your bookstore app needs to find all users based in California. When your app sends that query, rather than scanning the entire collection at random, MongoDB takes a more strategic approach. It first consults its query planner, which acts as an internal strategist. The query planner examines your query, checks what indexes are available, and picks the most efficient execution path. That path might use a single index, merge multiple indexes, or, in less ideal cases, scan the entire collection.

Once the plan is in place, MongoDB's execution engine takes over. It scans through documents or index entries, applies filters, performs sorting if needed, and returns only the matching documents: nothing more, nothing less.

Underneath it all lies the storage engine. By default, MongoDB uses the WiredTiger storage engine, a high-performance engine tailored for modern workloads. WiredTiger is responsible for how data is written to and retrieved from a disk. It takes care of the following:

- Compression to reduce storage size
- Encryption at rest to keep data secure
- A memory cache to speed up access to frequently used data
- Journaling (via a write-ahead log) to ensure data isn't lost during a crash or unexpected shutdown

This layered system, that is, the query planner, execution engine, and storage engine, means MongoDB can handle everything from simple reads to complex analytics. It gives you performance, reliability, and flexibility, whether you're building a small bookstore app or a high-traffic global platform.

# Distributed by design

MongoDB wasn't retrofitted for scale; it was built for it from the start. From its earliest versions, MongoDB was designed to handle large volumes of data and the realities of distributed computing. That's why features such as high availability and horizontal scaling aren't optional add-ons, but rather baked into the architecture via replica sets and sharding.

## Replica sets: Built-in high availability

At the core of MongoDB's resilience is the **replica set**. Picture a small team of servers working in harmony. One server, the **primary**, takes the lead, handling all write operations. The others, **secondaries**, continuously replicate their data, standing by in case something goes wrong.

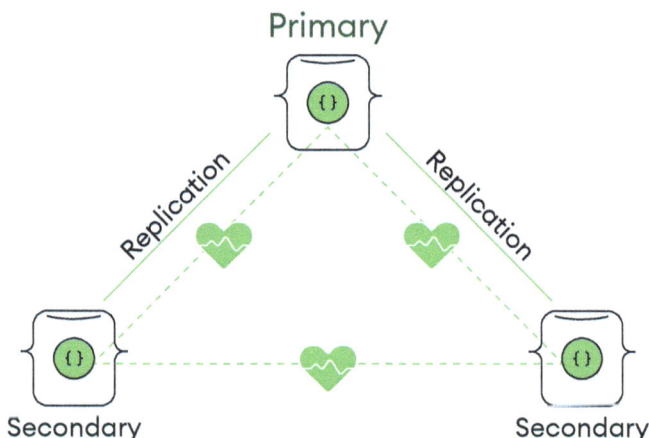

*Figure 1.1: A MongoDB replica set*

If the primary server fails, MongoDB automatically promotes one of the secondary servers to take over. This process takes place without manual intervention, ensuring your application continues to run and your data remains protected. This **automatic failover** capability means your database cluster can recover independently, reducing the need for constant monitoring.

## Sharding: Scaling horizontally

Imagine your bookstore app grows considerably. It's no longer just a local favorite; it's a global hit. Your catalog has ballooned to billions of books, reviews, orders, and users. At some point, one server simply won't be able to keep up. That's where sharding comes in.

**Sharding** is MongoDB's approach to horizontal scaling. It splits your data across multiple machines based on a **shard key**, a field that determines how documents are distributed. Each shard operates as its own replica set, giving you both scalability and redundancy in a single architecture.

*Figure 1.2* highlights the main components of the sharding architecture: the application, the mongos router, the config server, and the shards. The application interacts with a sharded cluster through mongos, which receives queries and routes them to the appropriate shard(s). The config server stores the metadata about the sharded cluster, such as the shard key.

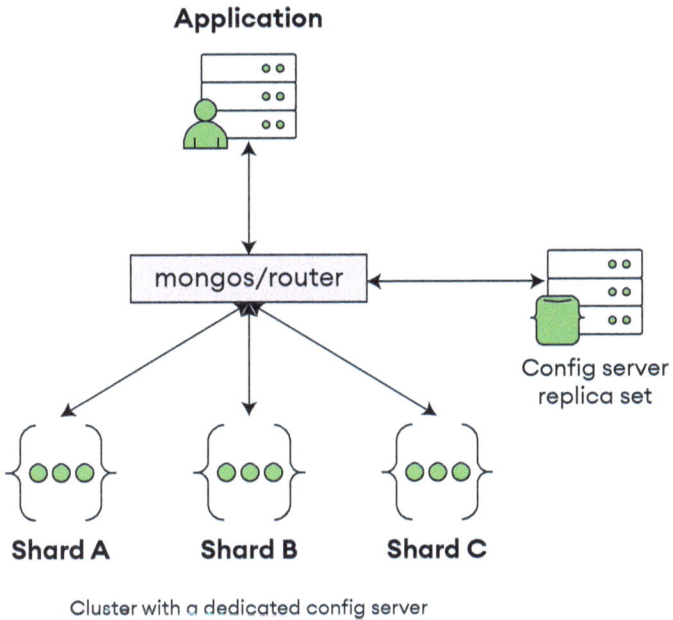

*Figure 1.2: High-level architecture of a sharded MongoDB cluster*

Your application interacts with MongoDB through a single, unified interface. MongoDB handles the complexity behind the scenes, routing queries, distributing data, and balancing the load.

## Working with data in MongoDB

Working with data is at the core of nearly every application, and MongoDB is built to make that experience intuitive, flexible, and powerful. Whether you're querying documents, writing code in your favorite language, or deploying in the cloud, MongoDB offers a developer-friendly approach to interacting with data. In this section, we'll walk through how querying works, how client libraries simplify integration, and how Atlas brings MongoDB to the cloud with ease.

## Operators: Expressive, JSON-based queries

At the heart of working with data is the simple act of *retrieving the information you need.*

If you're familiar with SQL, you might think of queries as the MongoDB equivalent of `SELECT ... WHERE`. But in MongoDB, queries are expressed using JSON-style syntax, making them feel more like expressions in a programming language than traditional SQL clauses.

At the core of every MongoDB query is an **operator**, a JSON object that describes what you're looking for.

Let's say your `books` collection contains the following two documents:

```
{
  title: "Learning MongoDB",
  author: "Alice",
  pages: 320,
  inStock: true,
  genres: ["Tech", "Database"]
}

{
  title: "Advanced Database Design",
  author: "Alice",
  pages: 450,
  inStock: false,
  genres: ["Tech", "Design"]
}
```

To find **all books**, regardless of their content, you can use an empty filter by running the following query:

```
db.books.find({})
```

To find only the books that are currently in stock, use this query:

```
db.books.find({ inStock: true })
```

In this case, the filter criteria `{ inStock: true }` is telling MongoDB, *"Give me every document where the* `inStock` *field is* `true`." Based on the sample data, the query will return the following document:

```
{
  title: "Learning MongoDB",
  author: "Alice",
  pages: 320,
  inStock: true,
  genres: ["Tech", "Database"]
}
```

You can also query based on any other field. For example, to find all books written by Alice, you can run the following:

```
db.books.find({ author: "Alice" })
```

This query returns both documents, since they share the same author value.

We'll dive into the full power of query operators in *Chapter 4*, *CRUD Operations*. For now, it's enough to understand that MongoDB uses JSON-style syntax to express your intent, and that makes querying in MongoDB both powerful and intuitive.

## Developer experience: Client libraries that speak your language

MongoDB provides official drivers for almost every language: Python, JavaScript, Go, Java, C#, Rust, and more. These drivers handle BSON encoding and decoding, manage connection pools and retry logic, and translate native syntax into the MongoDB wire protocol.

Here's an example of using the Python driver to connect to the MongoDB server, access the books collection in a bookstore database, and insert a new book document:

```python
from pymongo import MongoClient

client = MongoClient("mongodb://localhost:27017/")
db = client["bookstore"]
books = db["books"]
books.insert_one({
    "title": "Designing with Documents",
    "authors": [{"name": "Alex Kim"}],
    "publishedYear": 2024,
    "genres": ["Database", "Design"],
    "reviews": [
        {"reviewer": "Jamie", "rating": 5, "comment": "Clear and
practical."}
    ]
})
```

MongoDB returns the document as a native Python dictionary; no **object relational mapper** (**ORM**) is required. For example, the query for retrieving a book might look like this:

```python
result = books.find_one({"title": "Designing with Documents"})
print(result)
```

The query will return the following document:

```
{
    "_id": ObjectId("60f7e7a4e1b4f9b1c8fcb5b2"),
    "title": "Designing with Documents",
    "authors": [{"name": "Alex Kim"}],
    "publishedYear": 2024,
    "genres": ["Database", "Design"],
    "reviews": [
        {"reviewer": "Jamie", "rating": 5, "comment": "Clear and
practical."}
    ]
}
```

To learn more about all available client libraries, visit the MongoDB documentation:
https://www.mongodb.com/docs/drivers/.

## MongoDB fully managed in the cloud: Atlas

Everything you've read so far applies whether you're running MongoDB locally or in the cloud. Atlas is MongoDB's fully managed database service, designed to simplify deployment, scaling, and security. It also unlocks advanced capabilities such as Atlas Search and Atlas Vector Search.

Atlas makes it easy to spin up clusters, monitor performance, and manage backups without manual setup. For developers working locally or in automation workflows, the Atlas CLI provides full control of your cloud environments from the terminal, which is ideal for scripting and CI/CD pipelines.

We'll explore Atlas-specific features and tools throughout this book.

## Summary

In this chapter, you learned the fundamentals of MongoDB's architecture, including the document model, indexes, mongod, operators, replica sets, and sharding. MongoDB doesn't try to reinvent databases from scratch. Instead, it reimagines them to fit the realities of cloud-native, high-scale, iterative application development. MongoDB's architecture makes it a unique hybrid offering: as powerful as relational systems, as flexible as NoSQL, and as intuitive as your application model.

In the next chapter, you'll set up your local environment, connect to MongoDB using the shell, and run your first real commands.

To learn more about topics covered in this chapter, check out our relevant Skill Badges at MongoDB University and earn a credential:

### Relational to Document Model

Understand the shift from relational databases to MongoDB's document model.

`https://mdb.link/badge-relational-to-document`

### Indexing Design Fundamentals

Apply indexing strategies, optimize indexes for performance, and measure index performance.

`https://mdb.link/badge-indexing`

### Sharding Strategies

Explore shard keys, balancing, and distributed systems design.

`https://mdb.link/badge-sharding`

# 2

# Getting Started with MongoDB

Welcome to MongoDB. In this chapter, we'll start with the basics, getting MongoDB up and running on your system. Whether you're completely new to databases or transitioning from a relational background, this chapter will give you the foundation you need to follow along with the rest of the book.

Throughout this book, you'll find practical examples and code snippets you can run on your own. To make the most of these examples, it helps to have a local environment set up and ready to go. This chapter walks through installing MongoDB, creating a local deployment, connecting to it, and performing a simple operation, just enough to get your hands on the keyboard and start exploring.

In this chapter, you will do the following:

- Set up a local MongoDB instance using the MongoDB Atlas CLI
- Connect to the instance using the MongoDB Shell
- Verify that everything is working by running a basic read operation

The goal here is simple: get a working shell connected to a MongoDB instance so you can start exploring data. Let's get your environment ready, so you can hit the ground running in the chapters that follow.

## Installing the required tools

This setup relies on two main components: the MongoDB Atlas CLI and Docker. The command-line interface (CLI) manages the deployment, while Docker is responsible for running MongoDB inside a container. To follow along, you will need to have a few tools installed on your machine:

- Atlas CLI, the primary tool for managing your deployment
- mongosh, or the MongoDB Shell, for interacting with the database
- Docker, which provides a containerized environment to run MongoDB behind the scenes

If you're using macOS, the simplest way to install MongoDB tools is through Homebrew, which is available at https://brew.sh.

Open your terminal and run the following commands:

```
brew install mongodb-atlas-cli
brew install mongosh
brew install mongodb-compass  # Optional GUI
```

Make sure you also have Docker Desktop installed (version 4.31 or higher for macOS/Windows). On Linux, use Docker Engine version 27.0 or higher, or alternatively, Podman version 5.0 or higher. See https://docs.docker.com/desktop/ for more information and instructions for installation.

## Creating a local deployment

With the CLI installed and Docker running, it's time to start MongoDB. Follow these steps to create a local deployment:

1.  Open your terminal and run the following command:

    ```
    atlas deployments setup
    ```

    This launches an interactive setup process.

2.  When prompted, you'll see a message similar to the following one in your terminal. Select **local - Local Database**:

    ```
    ? What type of deployment would you like to work with?  [Use
    arrows to move, type to filter, ? for more help]
    > local - Local Database
      atlas - Atlas Database
    ```

3.  Next, you'll be asked how you want to set up your Atlas deployment, similar to the following message. Choose **default - With default settings** to quickly deploy a single-node replica set:

    ```
    ? How do you want to set up your local Atlas deployment?  [Use
    arrows to move, type to filter]
    > default - With default settings
      custom - With custom settings
      cancel - Cancel setup
    ```

4. In a few moments, you'll see a message like this:

```
Deployment created!
Connection string: mongodb://
localhost:27017/?directConnection=true
```

5. Next, the Atlas CLI will ask you how you want to connect to your MongoDB instance with the following options. Select **mongosh – MongoDB Shell**.

```
? How would you like to connect to local130?
> mongosh  -  MongoDB Shell
  compass  -  MongoDB Compass
  vscode   -  MongoDB for VS Code
  skip     -  Skip Connection
```

This will launch the MongoDB Shell and connect you directly to your newly running instance. From here, you're ready to start interacting with the database.

## Creating a database and collection

Let's create a simple database and collection, and then insert a sample document to verify that everything works as expected:

1. First, select the `bookstore` collection by running the following command in your terminal:

```
use bookstore
```

2. Next, run the following command to create a new collection called `books` and insert a document representing a book:

```
db.books.insertOne({title: "The Art of Indexing", author:
"Jane", pages: 220, inStock: true, genres: ["Tech",
"Databases"]})
```

You should see a message similar to the following if this operation was successful:

```
{
  acknowledged: true,
  insertedId: ObjectId('68823d1b272d5c8a92ed9d0b')
}
```

3.  Finally, query the collection to find and display all books that are currently in stock by running the following command:

```
db.books.find({ inStock: true }).pretty()
```

If successful, this will return the document we previously inserted:

```
[
  {
    _id: ObjectId('68823d1b272d5c8a92ed9d0b'),
    title: 'The Art of Indexing',
    author: 'Jane',
    pages: 220,
    inStock: true,
    genres: [ 'Tech', 'Databases' ]
  }
]
```

This confirms that your environment is fully operational and gives you a working shell for the rest of this book.

> **Tip**
>
> In MongoDB, there's no need to explicitly define schemas or structures upfront. Databases and collections are created automatically when you first insert data into them.

## Summary

You now have MongoDB running locally and are connected via the MongoDB Shell. This environment will support all the examples in the rest of this book.

In the next chapter, we'll start exploring how MongoDB structures data, and how to model it effectively using documents and collections.

# 3

# Data Modeling

If you've worked with relational databases, you already understand many of the fundamentals of schema design and data modeling in MongoDB. MongoDB uses many of the same principles, such as entities, attributes, and relationships, but applies them differently within a document-based model. The key idea here is *data that is accessed together should be stored together*.

This chapter will cover the following topics:

- How to identify entities in your data model
- How to model relationships between entities
- When to embed data versus when to reference it
- How to shift your thinking from tables and joins to documents and collections

Whether you're designing your first schema or refining an existing one, understanding how MongoDB structures data will help you create models that are not only efficient but also intuitive and aligned with your application's access patterns. This shift in thinking is critical for getting the most out of MongoDB's flexibility and performance.

## Thinking in documents: A practical mindset shift

Before diving into MongoDB's schema design, it will help to take a step back and identify the *what* and *why* of your data.

Before designing your schema, it helps to identify the core entities your application deals with and how they relate to one another. The following diagram illustrates these entities and their key relationships in the context of a bookstore.

# Entities

# Relationships

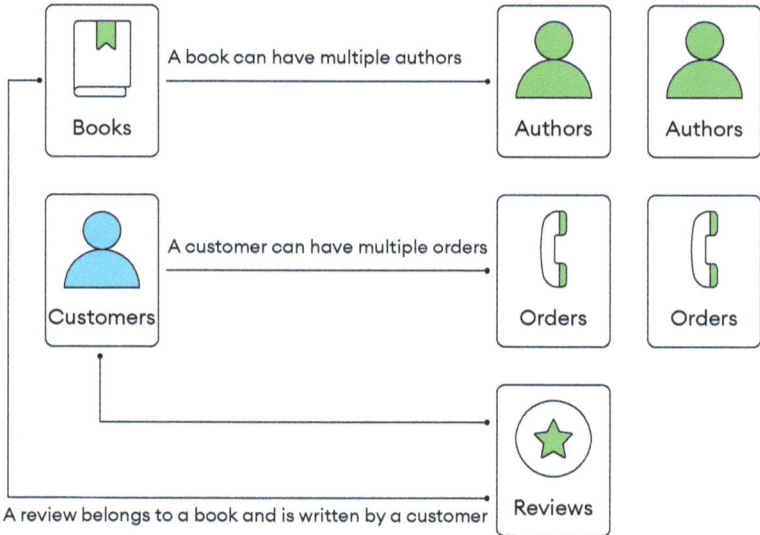

A book can have multiple authors

A customer can have multiple orders

A review belongs to a book and is written by a customer

*Figure 3.1: Key entities and relationships in a bookstore domain model*

This exercise may sound like classic relational modeling, and it is, because the fundamentals haven't changed. What does change in MongoDB is how you represent those relationships once you start thinking in terms of documents, not rows.

With entities and relationships in mind, you're now ready to explore how to translate them into a document model using embedding, referencing, and thoughtful data structure choices.

## Understanding schema design with the document model

By now, you know that MongoDB stores data in documents, which are JSON-like structures that represent individual entities. A document typically represents one entity, such as a book, an author, or a customer. Documents are grouped into collections, which serve as logical containers for related data.

MongoDB does not require a fixed schema. This gives you the flexibility to store similar data with different shapes in the same collection. This schema flexibility is one of MongoDB's defining features, allowing you to evolve your data model as your application grows.

But this flexibility doesn't mean chaos. MongoDB supports schema validation, allowing you to apply rules where structure matters. Moreover, MongoDB schema validation is built on JSON Schema, so you can define document structures using a widely adopted, standardized format. Using JSON Schema, you can enforce the presence of fields, constrain data types, or define nested document structures. In other words, MongoDB provides control where you need it, and freedom where you don't.

This model is supported by four core design principles:

- **Polymorphism**: Documents in the same collection can have different fields and structures. This flexibility lets you store diverse data types without forcing uniformity.
- **Arrays**: Fields can contain multiple values, including nested documents, allowing the natural representation of lists and relationships.
- **Embedding**: You can nest related data directly within a parent document, keeping everything tightly coupled and efficient to retrieve.
- **Referencing**: When data is shared, grows independently, or needs modularity, use references, typically via `_id`, to relate documents across collections.

Now that you understand the fundamentals of schema design, let's take a closer look at how MongoDB represents data relationships, which we'll discuss in more detail later. The choice between embedding documents and using references is central to this process, and it differs significantly from how relationships are handled in traditional relational databases.

## Embedding versus referencing

Relational databases rely on joins to reconstruct normalized data from multiple tables. MongoDB takes a different path. This isn't a limitation but a performance-conscious decision. Joins are expensive to scale, especially in distributed systems. Instead of normalizing everything and reconstructing it with joins, MongoDB encourages you to design schemas based on your application's data access and retrieval patterns.

In place of joins, MongoDB supports two core approaches:

- **Embedding** related data directly inside documents. For example, instead of joining an `authors` table with a `book` table, a MongoDB document might simply store the relevant `authors` details directly within each `book` document.

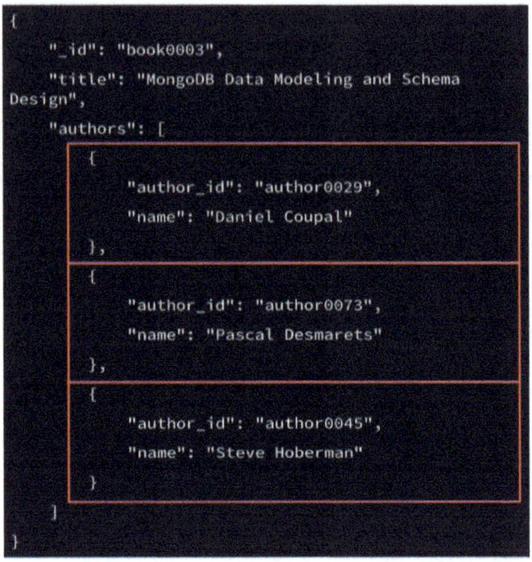
{
"_id": "book0003",
"title": "MongoDB Data Modeling and Schema Design",
"authors": [
{
"author_id": "author0029",
"name": "Daniel Coupal"
},
{
"author_id": "author0073",
"name": "Pascal Desmarets"
},
{
"author_id": "author0045",
"name": "Steve Hoberman"
}
]
}

*Figure 3.2: Author details embedded in a book document*

- **Referencing** documents by their unique `_id`, with follow-up queries in application logic. For instance, a book document might store an `authorId` value to retrieve author details separately when needed.

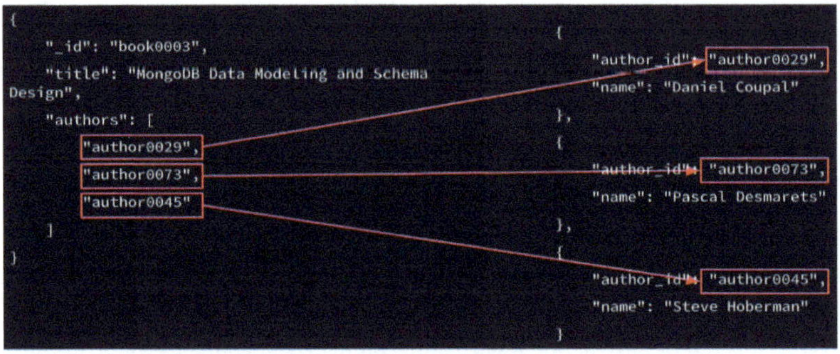
{
"_id": "book0003",
"title": "MongoDB Data Modeling and Schema Design",
"authors": [
"author0029",
"author0073",
"author0045"
]
}
{
"author_id": "author0029",
"name": "Daniel Coupal"
},
{
"author_id": "author0073",
"name": "Pascal Desmarets"
},
{
"author_id": "author0045",
"name": "Steve Hoberman"
}

*Figure 3.3: Author details stored in a separate document, which is referenced in the book document*

This results in simpler queries, fewer database round-trips, and easier scalability.

So, when do you use embedding, and when should you opt for referencing? This is an important decision you'll make in schema design: do you embed related data directly inside a document, or store it separately and reference it?

Embedding keeps everything in one place. It's fast, simple, and ideal in the following instances:

- The related data is always or usually accessed with the parent
- The embedded content doesn't grow unbounded
- The data is specific to that document and not shared elsewhere

Here's an example of embedding in the `books` collection, where author names are stored within a  printed book document:

```
{
  "_id": "book0003",
  "title": "MongoDB Data Modeling and Schema Design",
  "authors": [
    {
      "name": "Daniel Coupal"
    },
    {
      "name": "Pascal Desmarets"
    },
    {
      "name": "Steve Hoberman"
    }
  ]
}
```

In this example, if the application often retrieves a book along with its authors, embedding them together in the same document improves performance and simplifies queries.

Referencing, on the other hand, stores related data in separate documents, adding a layer of complexity because you need an additional query to retrieve it. However, it promotes modular design by keeping related entities separate and easier to manage independently. Use referencing in the following instances:

- The related data is large or frequently updated independently
- The related data is reused across multiple documents
- You want to prevent a single document from growing too large

Let's look at another example from the `books` collection. Here, a set of author IDs references separate author documents:

```
{
    "_id": "book0003",
    "title": "MongoDB Data Modeling and Schema Design",
    "authors": [
        "author0029",
        "author0073",
        "author0045"
    ]
}
```

Each author `_id` value corresponds to a document in a separate `authors` collection:

```
{
  "_id": "author0029",
  "name": "Daniel Coupal",
  "bio": "Author and data modeling expert..."
}
```

This approach allows you to update an author's details, for example, `bio`, without modifying any book documents that the author appears in.

To decide whether to embed or reference, it helps to first understand the type of relationship you're modeling. Let's explore how MongoDB represents relationships.

# Understanding relationships in MongoDB

MongoDB supports the same types of relationships you might design in a relational database: one-to-one, one-to-many, and many-to-many. But instead of relying only on the idea of foreign keys and joins, MongoDB gives you flexible options to model these relationships directly in your documents using embedding or referencing. The key is understanding which approach fits best for how your application accesses and updates data.

## One-to-one

One-to-one relationships are straightforward. A single document is associated with exactly one other. In MongoDB, this is often modeled by embedding.

Take the example of a publisher and its headquarters. Each publisher has exactly one headquarters address.

# One-to-One

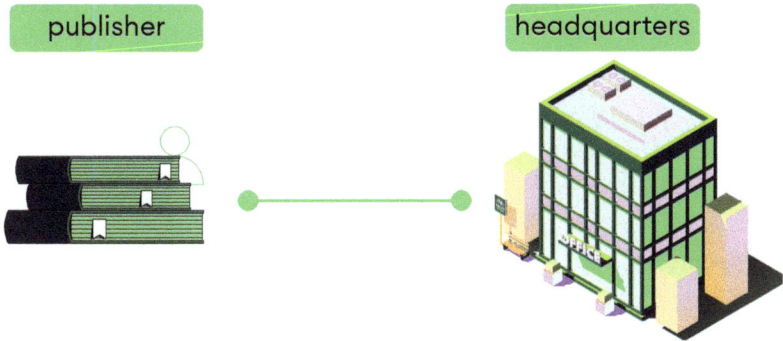

*Figure 3.4: A one-to-one relationship between a publisher and its headquarters*

In relational terms, these might be separate tables with a foreign key between them. In MongoDB, you have options.

If the headquarters information is small and always accessed with the publisher, you can embed the fields directly in the document:

```
{
    "_id": "publisher00023",
    "name": "MongoDB Press",
    "street": "1234 Ave",
    "city": "New York",
    "state": "New York",
    "country": "US",
    "zip": "10001"
}
```

To keep things organized, especially if the address structure varies by country, you might choose to group these fields into a subdocument:

```
{
    "_id": "publisher00023",
    "name": "MongoDB Press",
    "headquarters": {
        "street": "1234 Ave",
        "city": "New York",
        "state": "New York",
        "country": "US",
        "zip": "10001"
    }
}
```

If the headquarters data is large or managed independently, for example, updated by a different service, it may make more sense to reference it. You can place the reference in the parent:

```
{
  "_id": "publisher00023",
  "name": "MongoDB Press",
  "hq_id": "B72398845"
}
```

Or, you can place it in the child:

```
{
  "_id": "B72398845",
  "publisher_id": "publisher00023",
  "street": "1234 Ave",
  ...
}
```

You can also do both, that is bidirectional references, for applications that navigate in both directions frequently.

**Recommendation**

Embedding is usually best for tightly coupled data that is read together. Reference when the child is large, shared, or independently accessed.

## One-to-many

One-to-many is perhaps the most common pattern. In this pattern, a single entity is associated with two or more other entities.

# One-to-Many

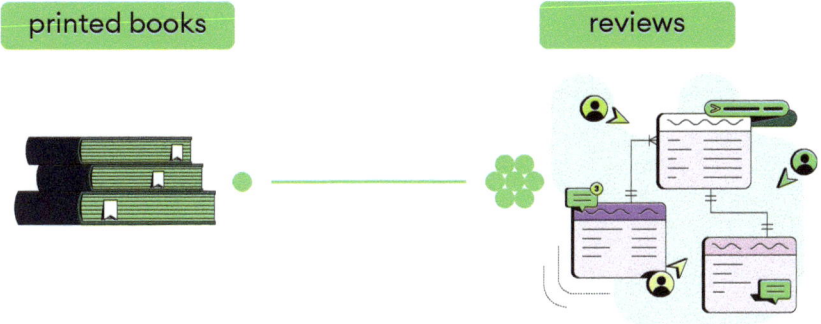

*Figure 3.5: A one-to-many relationship between a book and its reviews*

For example, a single book may have many reviews. In a relational model, this might mean separate tables and a join. In MongoDB, the simplest approach is to embed the *many* side directly within the *one*:

```
{
  "_id": "book001",
  "title": "MongoDB in Practice",
  "reviews": [
    {
      "reviewer": "Tanya",
      "rating": 5,
      "comment": "Great examples!"
    },
    {
      "reviewer": "Liam",
      "rating": 4,
      "comment": "Helpful but could use more visuals."
    }
  ]
}
```

This is fast and efficient, especially if reviews are always fetched alongside the book. There's no need for joins or additional queries.

Sometimes, instead of a flat array, you may group reviews into a subdocument with unique keys. This can offer more control or custom indexing:

```
{
  "_id": "book001",
  "title": "MongoDB in Practice",
  "reviews": {
    "user001": {
      "rating": 5,
      "comment": "Great examples!"
    },
    "user102": {
      "rating": 4,
      "comment": "Helpful but could use more visuals."
    }
  }
}
```

This pattern is less common but can be useful when each reviewer is uniquely identified and quick access by key is important.

But what if your reviews grow unbounded? A bestseller might accumulate tens of thousands. In that case, embedding can lead to oversized documents and degraded performance. That's when referencing makes more sense.

You can store an array of `review_ids` in the book:

```
{
  "_id": "book001",
  "review_ids": ["rev001", "rev002", ...]
}

Or have each review reference its parent book:
{
  "_id": "rev001",
  "book_id": "book001",
  "reviewer": "Tanya",
  ...
}
```

If needed, both sides can reference each other.

> **Recommendation**
>
> Embed when the *many* side is bounded and always accessed with the parent.
> Reference when it's large, independently accessed, or likely to grow over time.

## Many-to-many

Many-to-many relationships are the most complex, but also the most powerful. A book can
have multiple authors, and each author can write many books.

*Figure 3.6: A many-to-many relationship between a book and its authors*

In a relational schema, this would usually involve a join table. In MongoDB, you get to decide:
*embed* or *reference*?

If the author data is small and rarely changes, you might embed it directly into each book:

```
{
  "_id": "book023",
  "title": "Data Modeling with MongoDB",
  "authors": [
    {
      "name": "Daniel Coupal"
    },
    {
      "name": "Pascal Desmarets"
    }
  ]
}
```

This duplicates data (each author appears in multiple documents), but simplifies reads when fetching a book and its authors together; that is no need to query another collection. However, there's a trade-off: embedded authors aren't independent entities.

You can also use references. A book might store author IDs:

```
{
  "_id": "book023",
  "author_ids": ["auth001", "auth002"]
}
```

And authors can reference their books:

```
{
  "_id": "auth001",
  "name": "Daniel Coupal",
  "book_ids": ["book023", "book034"]
}
```

> **Recommendation**
>
> Embed when fast reads are a priority and duplication is acceptable. Reference when authors are shared, frequently updated, or accessed on their own.

## Final thoughts

Each relationship type in MongoDB gives you multiple modeling choices. The right one depends not just on structure but on your application's behavior as well:

- How often do you read the data together?
- Will parts of it grow without bounds?
- Is data shared across entities or unique to a parent?

Modeling in MongoDB isn't about following fixed rules. It's about making smart trade-offs, balancing simplicity, performance, and flexibility.

With these considerations in mind, the following table can be used as a general guide for deciding whether to embed or reference, based on some key design principles.

| Design guideline | Question | Embed | Reference |
|---|---|:---:|:---:|
| Simplicity | Would keeping the pieces of information together lead to a simpler data model and code? | ✓ | |
| Go together | Do the pieces of information have a has-a relationship, where one document owns or includes the other? | ✓ | |
| Query atomicity | Does the application query the pieces of information together? | ✓ | |
| Update complexity | Are the pieces of information updated independently? | | ✓ |
| Archival | Should the pieces of information be archived at different times? | | ✓ |
| Cardinality | Is there high or unbounded growth on the many side of the relationship? | | ✓ |
| Data duplication | Would data duplication be difficult to manage or risky? | | ✓ |
| Document size | Would combining the data exceed BSON limits or increase transfer cost? | | ✓ |
| Document growth | Will the embedded piece grow without bound, for example, a log or feed? | | ✓ |
| Write workload | Are the embedded elements written at different times, for example, comments or events? | | ✓ |

*Table 3.1: Guidelines for deciding when to embed or reference*

Choosing between embedding and referencing helps determine how you represent relationships in MongoDB. But modeling for performant often means going beyond relationship structure. In the next section, we'll discuss two strategies for optimizing data access: denormalization and arrays.

# Strategies for optimizing data access

We've covered the basics of data modeling in MongoDB. The concepts and strategies we've discussed will help you build efficient and performance applications. Now, we'll show you a few tips to further optimize your database design and minimize latency, reduce overhead, and ensure a seamless experience for your application's users.

## Using denormalization when modeling data

In MongoDB, denormalization, or copying small pieces of related data, is a common and encouraged strategy. While it may feel counterintuitive, especially if you come from a traditional relational database background where minimizing duplication is a key principle, denormalization is designed to optimize read performance and simplify data access. By embedding frequently accessed data directly within a document, you avoid costly `$lookup` operations and multiple round-trips to the database.

For example, let's return to our `books` collection, where each book is associated with a category. Instead of performing a separate query to retrieve the category name every time you retrieve a book, you can store the category name directly in the book document. This duplication eliminates the need to reference multiple collections at query time, streamlining reads.

In the following example, both `category_id` and `category_name` are stored within the book document. This approach means the application can access the category name immediately without an additional query:

```
{
  "_id": "book0421",
  "title": "Mastering Indexes in MongoDB",
  "category_id": "cat003",
  "category_name": "Database Design"
}
```

> **Note**
>
> If a category name changes, it can be updated across documents in bulk. But for most read-heavy use cases, denormalization simplifies access.

Now that you're aware of some of the advantages of using denormalization when modeling data, let's take a look at how the clever use of arrays when modeling data can further optimize your database design.

# Using arrays when modeling data

In relational databases, managing many-to-many relationships often involves multiple tables and join logic. But in MongoDB, you have two powerful native tools that let you model complex relationships directly within a document: arrays and embedded documents.

These aren't advanced features or hacks; they're fundamental parts of how you model data in MongoDB. Let's look at how they work, using examples from our `books` collection.

## Storing multiple values with arrays

Imagine a book that fits into several genres. In a relational model, this would usually require a separate genres table and a join table linking each book to its genres. In MongoDB, you simply use an array:

```
{
  _id: "book1021",
  title: "Understanding the Cosmos",
  genres: ["Science", "Astronomy", "Nonfiction"]
}
```

This structure lets you query books by genre just as easily. Here's an example:

```
db.books.find({ genres: "Science" })
```

MongoDB matches the value against elements in the array; no join tables needed. Arrays also adapt naturally as the number of related items grows or changes over time.

## Using arrays of embedded documents

Sometimes, you'll want to store an array of rich, structured values, that is, subdocuments that each contain multiple fields. For example, suppose your books contain the latest reviews, and each review includes a reviewer name, rating, and comment. Instead of modeling this in a separate collection, you can embed an array of subdocuments directly inside each book:

```
{
  _id: "book3105",
  title: "MongoDB in the Real World",
  reviews: [
    {
      reviewer: "Tanya",
      rating: 5,
      comment: "Great real-world examples."
    },
```

```
    {
      reviewer: "Liam",
      rating: 4,
      comment: "Clear and practical, but could use more diagrams."
    }
  ]
}
```

You can then query by fields inside the array:

```
db.books.find({ "reviews.reviewer": "Tanya" })
```

Arrays and embedded documents allow you to represent common patterns, such as one-to-many and many-to-many relationships, without needing joins. They align well with how most applications interact with data: you often need all the information about an entity in one go.

When used well, these structures do the following:

- Reduce the number of queries needed to assemble complete views
- Keep related data co-located for performance
- Make your schema easier to reason about

MongoDB doesn't just support these features; it encourages them as part of the document model's core design.

## Summary

Our goal in this chapter was to give you a foundation for thinking about data modeling in MongoDB: a MongoDB—a starting point, not a prescription. Modeling in a document-oriented system is different, but not unrecognizable if you're coming from a relational background. You'll still work with entities and relationships, but now with more choices: to embed or reference, to denormalize when it helps, and to structure your documents around how your application reads and writes data.

MongoDB gives you more flexibility and, with that, a bit more responsibility. There's no rigid schema to enforce structure for you; you decide what structure makes sense for your application. But in exchange, you get a model that fits your application, not the other way around. And here's the truth: you probably won't get it perfect on the first try, and that's okay. The document model is designed to evolve. What matters most is that you start modeling with intent that's guided by access patterns, not just database conventions.

The next chapter will cover the core operations every application needs: creating, reading, updating, and deleting documents in MongoDB.

To learn more about topics covered in this chapter, check out our relevant Skill Badges at MongoDB University and earn a credential:

### Relational to Document Model

Understand the shift from relational databases to MongoDB's document model.

https://mdb.link/badge-relational-to-document

### Schema Patterns and Anti-patterns

Model one-to-one, one-to-many, many-to-many relationships; apply embedding and referencing effectively; and denormalize and optimize schemas.

https://mdb.link/badge-patterns

# 4

# CRUD Operations

At the heart of working with data is the ability to **create**, **read**, **update**, and **delete** it: the four fundamental operations commonly referred to as **CRUD**.

MongoDB provides a rich and flexible API for performing these operations on documents. Because MongoDB uses a document model rather than tables and rows, CRUD operations are not only intuitive but also often more expressive than their SQL equivalents. They let you interact with nested structures, arrays, and dynamic schemas, all with concise and readable commands.

In this chapter, you'll learn how to do the following:

- Insert new documents
- Query existing data
- Modify parts of a document
- Remove documents from a collection

As in the previous chapters, we'll use the familiar bookstore example throughout, with collections such as `books`, `authors`, and `reviews`.

## Inserting documents

To insert data in MongoDB, you write documents to a collection. You don't need to define a schema in advance; MongoDB will create the collection automatically if it doesn't exist.

To insert a new book into the `books` collection, use the `insertOne` command:

```
db.books.insertOne({
  title: "Designing with Documents",
  authors: [{ name: "Alex Kim" }],
  publishedYear: 2024,
  genres: ["Database", "Design"],
  publisher: {
    name: "Schema Free Press",
    location: "San Francisco"
  }
});
```

MongoDB automatically assigns a unique `_id` field to each document if you don't provide one.

To insert multiple books at once, you use `insertMany`:

```
db.books.insertMany([
  {
    title: "MongoDB Basics",
    authors: [{ name: "Chris Doe" }],
    publishedYear: 2023
  },
  {
    title: "Schema Evolution",
    authors: [{ name: "Jordan Lane" }],
    publishedYear: 2022
  }
]);
```

As you probably guessed, `insertMany()` is the preferred method for inserting multiple documents into your database at the same time. When you use `insertMany()`, MongoDB combines the documents into a single batch operation. This minimizes network overhead and reduces the number of round-trips to the database.

## Reading documents

The `find()` method in MongoDB allows you to query your database in powerful and flexible ways.

For example, to return all documents in a collection, use the following command:

```
db.books.find();
```

To find books in the `"Design"` genre, you can add a condition like this:

```
db.books.find({ genres: "Design" });
```

To return only specific fields, for example, the title and authors, you can use a projection:

```
db.books.find(
  { genres: "Design" },
  { title: 1, authors: 1, _id: 0 }
);
```

MongoDB queries support a wide range of operations, including the following:

- Logical operators such as `$and`, `$or`, and `$not`
- Comparison operations such as `$gt`, `$lt`, and `$in`

- Access to nested fields using dot notation (e.g., `"publisher.name"`)
- Array-specific queries using operators such as `$elemMatch`

You can also sort and limit the results of a query. For example, the following command returns the five most recently published books:

```
db.books.find().sort({ publishedYear: -1 }).limit(5);
```

Reading documents is often the first step in building your application's data view, whether it's for listing search results, filtering content, or preparing a UI page.

# Updating documents

MongoDB updates documents using the `updateOne()` and `updateMany()` methods. These methods allow you to modify specific parts of a document using update operators.

For example, to add a `pageCount` field to a single book, you can use the following command:

```
db.books.updateOne(
  { title: "Designing with Documents" },
  { $set: { pageCount: 288 } }
);
```

If you want to update all books from a specific publisher, you can use the `updateMany()` method:

```
db.books.updateMany(
  { "publisher.name": "Schema Free Press" },
  { $set: { publisherType: "Independent" } }
);
```

You can update array fields too. For instance, to add a new review to a book's reviews array, you can use the `$push` operator:

```
db.books.updateOne(
  { title: "Designing with Documents" },
  {
    $push: {
      reviews: {
        reviewer: "Jamie",
        rating: 5,
        comment: "Incredibly practical and clear!"
      }
    }
  }
);
```

To update a specific review in the array, such as changing Jamie's rating, you can use the positional $ operator:

```
db.books.updateOne(
  { title: "Designing with Documents", "reviews.reviewer": "Jamie" },
  { $set: { "reviews.$.rating": 4 } }
);
```

MongoDB also gives you the option to replace entire documents. To do this, use replaceOne():

```
db.books.replaceOne(
  { title: "MongoDB Basics" },
  {
    title: "MongoDB Basics - 2nd Edition",
    authors: [{ name: "Chris Doe" }],
    publishedYear: 2025
  }
);
```

This command removes any fields not included in the new document, so use it with care.

When updating or replacing documents, make sure you use the correct filter criteria, so you only update the fields or documents you want, to avoid any nasty surprises. You could test your update or replace operations by first running a find() query with the same filter.

## Deleting documents

Finally, MongoDB also allows you to delete documents using the deleteOne() and deleteMany() methods. These methods allow you to delete a document or documents that match the specified condition. When using deleteOne(), note that only the first document that matches the condition will be removed, even if multiple documents meet the condition.

To remove a single document, use the following:

```
db.books.deleteOne({ title: "Schema Evolution" });
```

To delete multiple documents matching a condition, use the following:

```
db.books.deleteMany({ publishedYear: { $lt: 2020 } });
```

The deleteOne() and deleteMany() methods are powerful tools, so use them carefully. Always use a filter criterion to ensure you only remove the documents you want. For example, running deleteMany() without any filter criteria will delete all documents in the collection. To avoid this, you could test your delete operations by first running a find() query with the same filter.

# Summary

CRUD operations in MongoDB are simple but powerful. They give you direct control over your data using expressive queries and flexible update patterns. Whether you're working with deeply nested structures, arrays, or evolving schemas, CRUD is your first tool for interacting with MongoDB's document model.

In the next chapter, we'll dive deeper into data transformation and querying with the aggregation framework, MongoDB's answer to advanced data analysis.

To learn more about topics covered in this chapter, check out our relevant Skill Badges at MongoDB University and earn a credential:

**CRUD Operations in MongoDB**

Perform CRUD operations, design effective queries, and modify query results.

https://mdb.link/badge-crud

# 5

# Aggregation

MongoDB's aggregation framework lets you go beyond simple data retrieval; you can transform, filter, group, and summarize your data with ease. Think of MongoDB's aggregation framework as a data transformation *pipeline*, with documents passing through a series of stages. Now, imagine running your bookstore's entire sales history through this pipeline. At each stage, the data is filtered, reshaped, or summarized until it emerges as exactly what you need: top-selling genres, customer purchase trends, or average ratings by author.

This chapter will cover the following topics:

- The basics of aggregation in MongoDB
- Overview of different aggregation stages
- Example aggregation pipelines
- Aggregation and Atlas Search
- Tips for optimal performance

By the end of this chapter, you'll know how to shape your data into meaningful insights using MongoDB's powerful aggregation pipeline.

## Aggregation pipeline

An aggregation pipeline provides a structured way to transform, combine, and analyze documents within a collection. It is both modular and composable, allowing you to chain together multiple stages, each performing a specific transformation or operation on the documents it receives. The output of one stage becomes the input to the next.

If you're familiar with Unix-style commands, it's conceptually similar. Here is an example:

```
cat data.log | grep ERROR | sort | head -n 10
```

In MongoDB, the aggregation framework processes data through a series of stages, each transforming the documents as they pass through the pipeline. Some commonly used stages include the following:

- A `$match` stage to filter documents
- A `$group` stage to aggregate data
- A `$sort` stage to order the results
- A `$project` stage to reshape the output

The order of these stages matters. A well-structured pipeline typically begins with operations that reduce the amount of data early, improving performance downstream.

## Core building blocks

MongoDB provides a rich set of operators and expressions that allow you to build powerful transformations within the aggregation pipeline:

- **Stages** such as `$match`, `$group`, `$sort`, and `$project` define what each step in the pipeline does
- **Accumulator expressions** such as `$sum`, `$avg`, `$push`, and `$max` are used inside grouping stages to compute values across grouped documents
- **Path expressions** such as `"$field"` or `"$author.name"` let you reference fields in your documents
- **Conditional expressions** such as `$cond`, `$ifNull`, and `$switch` support logic-based transformations within the pipeline
- **System variables** such as `$$NOW` allow you to access runtime data, and `$$ROOT` allows you to reference the root document being processed in the pipeline stage

The aggregation syntax, like all other MongoDB queries, uses a JSON-like notation, but it takes it further by chaining multiple transformation stages. You'll still use the familiar $ symbol for operators and field paths, just like in queries such as `{ price: { $gt: 20 } }`, but now applied in a structured pipeline to reshape and compute documents step by step.

# Practical examples and patterns

Let's walk through three examples using a fictional sales collection from a bookstore.

# Example 1: Books sold by genre in 2024

This pipeline returns information about how many copies of each genre of book were sold in the year 2024. This is useful when trying to determine which genre was the most popular in a given year:

```
db.sales.aggregate([
    { $match: { year: 2024 } },
    { $unwind: "$books" },
    { $group: { _id: "$books.genre", totalSold: { $sum: 1 } } },
    { $project: { _id: 0, genre: "$_id", totalSold: 1 } },
    { $sort: { totalSold: -1 } }
])
```

Here's what each stage of the pipeline does:

- `$match`: Filters the collection to only include documents where the `year` field is 2024.
- `$unwind`: Deconstructs the `books` array from each document into individual documents.
- `$group`: Groups these documents by `genre` and counts the number of books sold in each genre. This produces the total number of books sold for each genre.
- `$project`: Reshapes the output to only include the `genre` and `totalSold` fields. This makes our results easier to read.
- `$sort`: Sorts the results by `totalSold` in descending order, so the genres that have sold the most appear at the top of the list.

This pipeline gives you a clear view of genre popularity, which is perfect for spotting trends and making data-driven decisions.

# Example 2: Top 10 highest-rated books since 2017

This pipeline returns information about the highest user-rated books since 2017. This can be useful if we want to recommend popular books to other users or track the popularity of certain books over time:

```
db.reviews.aggregate([
    { $match: { year: { $gte: 2017 } } },
    { $group: { _id: "$book_id", avgRating: { $avg: "$rating" } } },
    { $sort: { avgRating: -1 } },
    { $limit: 10 }
])
```

Here's what each stage of the pipeline does:

- $match: Filters the collection to only include reviews where the year field is greater than or equal to 2017
- $group: Groups the filtered reviews by book_id and calculates the average rating for each book
- $sort: Sorts the grouped results by avgRating in descending order
- $limit: Limits the output to the top 10 entries

By analyzing review trends over time, this query helps surface standout books that readers consistently love.

## Example 3: Join customers with their children's book purchases

In this pipeline, we're joining customer names and email addresses from the customers collection with our sales collection. This is helpful when we want to identify customers who have purchased books with a specific genre(Children in this example) and contact them with recommendations:

```
db.sales.aggregate([
  {
    $lookup: {
      from: "customers",
      localField: "customer_id",
      foreignField: "_id",
      as: "customer"
    }
  },
  { $unwind: "$customer" },
  { $set: {
    childrenBooks: {
      $filter: {
        input: "$books",
        as: "book",
        cond: { $eq: ["$$book.genre", "Children"] }
      }
    }
  }},
  { $match: { "childrenBooks.0": { $exists: true } } },
  { $project: { _id: 0, customer: 1, childrenBooks: 1 } }
])
```

Here's what each stage of the pipeline does:

- `$lookup`: Joins the `customers` collection with the `sales` collection, using `customer_id` in the `sales` collection and `_id` in the `customers` collection. This adds a new field called `customer` to the `sales` collection, which is an array containing the matching customer document(s).
- `$unwind`: Deconstructs the `customer` array created in the previous stage into individual documents for easier access.
- `$set`: Declares a new field, `childrenBooks`, using `$filter` to extract only books within the books array where the genre is `Children`. The result of this stage is that the `childrenBooks` field will contain an array of children books purchased in the sale.
- `$match`: Filters the results to include only sales where `childrenBooks` is not empty. In other words, the customer has purchased at least one book from the `Children` genre.
- `$project`: Reshapes the output to include only the `customer` and `childrenBooks` fields so the resulting document only contains the customer details and the book they purchased.

## Improving aggregation pipeline performance

Aggregation pipelines are efficient by design, but how you build them impacts performance. Keep these tips in mind when designing your pipelines:

- Filter early with `$match` and `$limit` to reduce the volume of data passed through the pipeline
- Use indexes on fields involved in `$match` or `$sort` stages to speed up retrieval
- Avoid unnecessary reshaping with early `$project` stages unless they help reduce payload
- Pair `$sort` with `$limit` for efficient top-N queries
- Work with arrays smartly; use `$map`, `$filter`, or `$reduce` instead of always relying on `$unwind`

MongoDB does a lot to optimize your pipeline automatically, but a thoughtful pipeline design ensures performance scales with your data.

# Aggregation and Atlas Search

Another powerful feature of the aggregation framework is how it integrates with Atlas Search. The `$search` stage is a first-class pipeline stage that lets you run full-text and semantic search directly within aggregation queries.

You can use $search when you want to do the following:

- Match on text fields using lexical rules (e.g., stemming and tokenization)
- Allow fuzzy matches to account for typos
- Combine multiple conditions with the compound operator
- Rank results by relevance with BM25 or vector similarity
- Return snippets of matching text for previews
- Run vector searches using semantic embeddings

> **Note**
>
> A search index must be created first in order for your search query to execute.

Here is an example using $search in a bookstore:

```
db.books.aggregate([
  {
    $search: {
      index: "titlePlotIndex",
      text: {
        query: "space exploration",
        path: ["title", "plot"],
        fuzzy: {}
      }
    }
  },
  { $limit: 5 },
  { $project: { title: 1, plot: 1, _id: 0, score: { $meta:
"searchScore" } } }
]);
```

The $search stage must be the first stage in your aggregation pipeline. From there, you can combine it with other stages, such as $match, $sort, $project, $facet, $lookup, or $set, to further shape your results.

# Summary

MongoDB's aggregation framework lets you reshape and analyze your data, from filtering and grouping to joining and computing. With its stage-based approach, it offers clarity, flexibility, and expressive control over your data transformations. But with great power comes the need for care; pipeline design, operator choices, and data flow all affect performance.

In the next chapter, we'll go deeper into those performance considerations.

To learn more about topics covered in this chapter, check out our relevant Skill Badges at MongoDB University and earn a credential:

**Fundamentals of Data Transformation**

Define aggregation framework, understand stage ordering, and build an aggregation pipeline.

https://mdb.link/badge-aggregation

# 6

# Performance Strategies and Tools

Now that we have gone over CRUD and aggregation, the next step is making sure our queries run fast, scale well, and don't overwhelm our system. MongoDB provides several tools and techniques to help you understand and improve performance, whether you're optimizing a single query or preparing your app for production at scale.

This chapter will cover the following topics:

- An overview of indexes and how they work in MongoDB
- Understanding query shape and the ESR guideline to help you build performant indexes
- Interpreting explain plans to determine whether your queries are using the correct indexes
- Assess the performance of your queries with the profiler
- Determine the index size and usage with stats and sizing

These strategies and tools will help you build efficient, scalable queries and maintain high performance as your application grows.

## Indexes

Indexes are data structures that improve the speed of read operations by allowing MongoDB to locate documents without scanning the entire collection. They are especially critical in read-heavy applications, where fast queries can make or break performance.

When you run a query such as `db.books.find({ author: "Alice" })`, MongoDB will scan the whole collection unless an index on the `author` field exists. With an index, it jumps directly to the matching documents, saving time, memory, and CPU.

MongoDB supports several types of indexes, each designed to improve query performance for different use cases.

To index a single field, for example, the `author` field, you would use the following:

```
db.books.createIndex({ author: 1 })
```

If you need to index multiple fields together, such as `genre` and `rating`, you can create a compound index like this:

```
db.books.createIndex({ genre: 1, rating: -1 })
```

To enforce uniqueness on a field such as `email`, here's how you can define a unique index:

```
db.customers.createIndex({ email: 1 }, { unique: true })
```

You can also index embedded fields. For example, to index the `publisher.name` field, which exists within a nested object inside the documents in the `books` collection, use the following:

```
db.books.createIndex({ "publisher.name": 1 })
```

Use indexes strategically by only indexing on fields you query or sort on frequently, as over-indexing can slow down write times.

# Performance analysis tools

To ensure your queries are efficient and your indexes are working as expected, MongoDB offers several built-in tools. These help you analyze how queries are executed, spot bottlenecks, and make data-driven indexing decisions.

## Query shape and the ESR guideline

A *query shape* is the combination of filters, sorts, and projections used in a query. MongoDB matches indexes based on shape, not just fields.

To design compound indexes that match your query shapes, follow the **ESR guideline**:

- Equality fields first
- Sort fields next
- Range fields last

For example, if your query filters by `author` (equality), sorts by `rating`, and filters a price range, a good index would be `{ author: 1, rating: 1, price: 1 }`.

## Explain plans

You can use the `.explain()` method to see how MongoDB is executing your queries. The `.explain()` method returns a detailed report, known as an explain plan, that shows whether indexes were used in the execution of a query, how many documents were examined, and how long the query took to run.

For example, to check the execution of a `find()` query, you can run the following command:

```
db.books.explain("executionStats").find({ author: "Alice" })
```

When reading the explain output, here are a few key indicators to focus on:

- `IXSCAN` indicates that an index was used, which is good
- `COLLSCAN` means a full collection scan occurred, which is typically slow
- `executionTimeMillis` shows how much time was spent processing
- `nReturned` vs `totalDocsExamined` shows the efficiency ratio

You can also analyse aggregation pipelines with `.explain()`, like so:

```
db.sales.explain("executionStats").aggregate([ { $match: { year: 2024
} } ])
```

This allows you to validate whether your pipeline stages and indexes are working together.

## The profiler

MongoDB includes a built-in profiler that records slow or resource-intensive operations. You can enable it with the following command:

```
db.setProfilingLevel(1, 100)   // logs queries taking longer than 100ms
```

To inspect the results, run the following:

```
db.system.profile.find().sort({ ts: -1 }).limit(5)
```

This will show you the query shape, how long the profiled queries took to execute, and how many documents were read. This is a great tool for catching performance regressions during development or QA, before they reach production.

## Stats and sizing

MongoDB includes quick stats for understanding the size and index usage of your collections and databases. To view collection-level stats, use the following:

```
db.books.stats()
```

For database-level stats, you can use the following:

```
db.stats()
```

These statistics help you understand collection size, index usage, and document counts. This is especially useful for spotting large collections or unused indexes or for planning migrations.

## Summary

MongoDB offers a powerful set of tools to monitor and optimize performance. Indexes speed up reads, explain plans show you how queries run, the profiler logs slow operations, and built-in stats reveal storage overhead. Using these tools strategically ensures MongoDB scales reliably and efficiently alongside your application.

The next chapter explores how MongoDB supports intelligent applications through full-text and semantic search, enabling AI-powered use cases such as RAG and agents.

To learn more about topics covered in this chapter, check out our relevant Skill Badges at MongoDB University and earn a credential:

**Indexing Design Fundamentals**

Apply indexing strategies, optimize indexes for performance, and measure index performance.

https://mdb.link/badge-indexing

**Performance Tools and Techniques**

Use tuning techniques (profiling and slow query analysis), optimize indexes and cache utilization.

https://mdb.link/badge-performance-tools

# 7

# Intelligent Applications with MongoDB

As AI capabilities expand, applications increasingly need to search, summarize, and reason over structured, semi-structured, and unstructured data. MongoDB provides two built-in tools to support this: Atlas Search for lexical relevance and Atlas Vector Search for semantic similarity. Combined, these make MongoDB a strong foundation for intelligent applications, such as **retrieval-augmented generation** (**RAG**) and AI agents, while keeping your data operational and contextually connected.

This chapter will cover the following topics:

- Lexical search and semantic search
- Using full-text search with Atlas Search
- Leveraging the power of AI with semantic search
- The basics of RAG and AI agents

This chapter illustrates how MongoDB's built-in search and AI capabilities can support intelligent applications.

## Lexical search with Atlas Search

For traditional full-text use cases, such as searching titles, filtering descriptions, or supporting autocomplete, MongoDB offers **Atlas Search**, which is built on Apache Lucene and integrated directly into the aggregation framework.

The first step in using Atlas Search is to create a search index on the fields you want to query, as in this example:

```
db.books.createSearchIndex("titlePlotIndex", {
  mappings: {
    dynamic: false,
    fields: {
      title: { type: "string" },
      plot: { type: "string" },
```

```
        published: { type: "date" }
      }
    }
  });
```

Here, we create an Atlas Search index on the `title`, `plot`, and `published` fields.

Once the index is created, you can use `$search` as the **first stage** in your aggregation to query with lexical operators:

```
db.books.aggregate([
  {
    $search: {
      index: "titlePlotIndex",
      text: {
        query: "alien encounter",
        path: ["title", "plot"],
        fuzzy: {}
      }
    }
  },
  { $limit: 5 },
  {
    $project: {
      _id: 0,
      title: 1,
      plot: 1,
      score: { $meta: "searchScore" }
    }
  }
]);
```

MongoDB Atlas Search uses a **relevancy algorithm** for ranking and supports autocomplete, highlighting, and compound queries. It integrates seamlessly with `$match`, `$sort`, `$facet`, `$project`, and other aggregation stages, making it easy to enrich results with other data.

## Semantic search with Atlas Vector Search

For semantic search, such as finding books with similar themes or retrieving relevant knowledge, MongoDB offers Atlas Vector Search.

While MongoDB supports any embedding model, Voyage AI is its purpose-built embedding model optimized for performance and search accuracy. It is designed for dense vector representation and integrated with Atlas. The first step in using Atlas Vector Search is to generate and store embeddings:

```
db.books.insertOne({
  title: "Space Legacy",
  summary: "A tale of astronauts building a new world",
  embedding: [0.017, -0.233, 0.942, ...] // Voyage AI embedding
});
```

Next, create a vector index on the embedding field:

```
db.books.createSearchIndex({
  definition: {
    fields: {
      embedding: {
        type: "vector",
        dims: 1536,
        similarity: "cosine"
      }
    }
  }
});
```

Finally, use the $vectorSearch stage within an aggregation pipeline to retrieve semantically similar documents:

```
db.books.aggregate([
  {
    $vectorSearch: {
      index: "vectorIndex",
      path: "embedding",
      queryVector: userQueryEmbedding,
      numCandidates: 100,
      limit: 3
    }
  },
  {
    $project: {
      title: 1,
      snippet: 1,
      score: { $meta: "vectorSearchScore" }
    }
  }
]);
```

You can also use pre-filters and projection stages such as $match or $project to shape the results or filter based on metadata, for example, by genre or publication year.

# Retrieval-augmented generation (RAG)

In a RAG pipeline, MongoDB stores both **operational** and **reference** data, which provides your LLM with additional context when answering user queries. When a user submits a query, the following steps are followed:

1. Their input is embedded into a dense vector.
2. A vector search retrieves the most relevant passages.
3. A language model generates a response using the retrieved context.

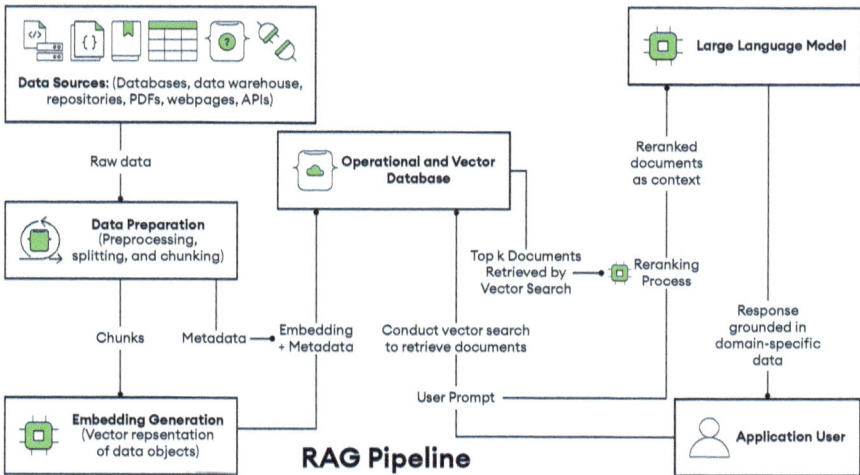

*Figure 7.1: End-to-end flow of a RAG-based application using vector search and LLMs*

MongoDB supports RAG by combining vector search and metadata filtering in a single query, as in this example:

```
db.books.aggregate([
  {
    $vectorSearch: {
      index: "bookEmbeddingIndex",
      path: "embedding",
      queryVector: userQueryEmbedding,
      numCandidates: 100,
      limit: 3,
      filter: { genre: "science fiction" }
    }
  },
```

```
  {
    $project: {
      title: 1,
      snippet: 1,
      score: { $meta: "vectorSearchScore" }
    }
  }
]);
```

With MongoDB, RAG is operationally efficient; there's no need to manage separate databases for vectors, metadata, or application state.

A typical RAG pipeline with MongoDB includes the following steps:

1. **Ingest**: Store PDFs, docs, and catalog data in a MongoDB collection.

2. **Embed**: Use Voyage AI to convert chunks into vector embeddings.

3. **Store**: Save the raw text, its embeddings, and related metadata in the same collection.

4. **Query**: Embed the user's input and retrieve contextually relevant data with `$vectorSearch`.

5. **Generate**: Pass the retrieved context to an **LLM** to answer user queries.

This unified approach simplifies infrastructure and accelerates development for generative AI applications.

# Agents and real-time context

AI agents reason, take actions, and use tools to complete complex tasks. MongoDB supports this by storing evolving user state, retrieved facts, and memory, all in one place. This unified context makes agent behavior more grounded, adaptive, and personalized.

In practice, this means the following:

- Chat agents remember user preferences across sessions
- Scheduling agents access calendars and task history from the same store
- Diagnostic bots analyze structured data (logs) and unstructured notes

MongoDB acts as both the memory and the knowledge base, enabling agents to operate with continuity and context. Whether it's recalling past queries, filtering based on metadata, or adapting to user behavior, agents built on MongoDB can think, learn, and evolve in real time.

# Summary

MongoDB brings AI readiness to your applications by combining traditional search, semantic retrieval, and real-time context in a single, unified platform. With Atlas Search and Atlas Vector Search, which is powered by embeddings from models such as Voyage AI, you  can build RAG pipelines, intelligent agents, and deeply contextual user experiences, all without moving data outside your operational database.

To learn more about topics covered in this chapter, check out our relevant Skill Badges at MongoDB University and earn a credential:

**Vector Search Fundamentals**

Understand semantic search, store embeddings, and perform a vector search.

https://mdb.link/badge-vector

**RAG with MongoDB**

Describe chunking strategies and create a RAG application.

https://mdb.link/badge-rag

**AI Agents with MongoDB**

Create multi-tool agents with MongoDB and define memory for an agent.

https://mdb.link/badge-agent

# Conclusion

By now, you've seen how MongoDB unlocks new ways of working with data, from its flexible document model and expressive queries to built-in scalability, performance tooling, and AI-ready search. MongoDB enables you to design systems that are adaptive, intuitive, and aligned with how modern applications are built and evolve.

This book gave you a practical foundation of how to model data based on real access patterns, scale reliably with replica sets and sharding, and extend your application with features such as full-text and vector search. In doing so, we hope you not only understand these features but also have developed a mindset that embraces agility, performance, and user-focused design.

But learning the concepts is just the beginning.

To turn that knowledge into validated capability, MongoDB offers **Skill Badges,** which are short, hands-on assessments that help you demonstrate and deepen your expertise. Whether you're running deployments, writing secure queries, designing schemas, or integrating AI, Skill Badges let you show what you know and know what to learn next.

Skill Badges are designed for a range of roles, from builders to operators, architects to analysts, so you and your teams can grow in sync, aligned around shared best practices.

If this book helped you gain clarity and confidence, Skill Badges are how you turn it into progress.

Explore the next steps and level up your MongoDB skills at `https://learn.mongodb.com/skills`.

# ‹packt›

packtpub.com

Subscribe to our online digital library for full access to over 7,000 books and videos, as well as industry leading tools to help you plan your personal development and advance your career. For more information, please visit our website.

## Why subscribe?

- Spend less time learning and more time coding with practical eBooks and Videos from over 4,000 industry professionals
- Improve your learning with Skill Plans built especially for you
- Get a free eBook or video every month
- Fully searchable for easy access to vital information
- Copy and paste, print, and bookmark content

At www.packtpub.com, you can also read a collection of free technical articles, sign up for a range of free newsletters, and receive exclusive discounts and offers on Packt books and eBooks.

.

# Other Books You May Enjoy

If you enjoyed this book, you may be interested in these other books by Packt:

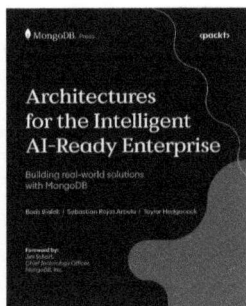

**Architectures for the Intelligent AI-Ready Enterprise**

Boris Bialek, Sebastian Rojas Arbulu, Taylor Hedgecock

ISBN: 978-1-80611-715-4

- Design AI-ready data architectures that scale in production
- Define systems of action and explain why they matter for enterprises
- Modernize legacy systems for AI-ready, unified architectures
- Implement governance, privacy, and compliance frameworks for AI
- Explore real-world AI implementations for over six industries
- Deploy production RAG and agentic systems with MongoDB
- Apply semantic data protection in regulated industries
- Build domain-specific AI agents and intelligent copilots
- Apply MCP, causal AI, and multi-agent systems for future-ready architectures

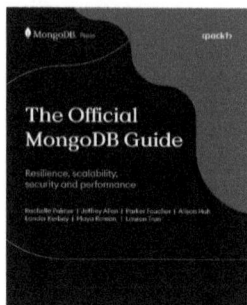

The Official MongoDB Guide

Rachelle Palmer, Jeffrey Allen, Parker Faucher, Alison Huh, Lander Kerbey, Maya Raman, Lauren Tran

ISBN: 978-1-83702-197-0

- Build secure, scalable, and high-performance applications
- Design efficient data models and indexes for real workloads
- Write powerful queries to sort, filter, and project data
- Protect applications with authentication and encryption
- Accelerate coding with AI-powered and IDE-based tools
- Launch, scale, and manage MongoDB Atlas with confidence
- Unlock advanced features like Atlas Search and Atlas Vector Search
- Apply proven techniques from MongoDB's own engineering leaders

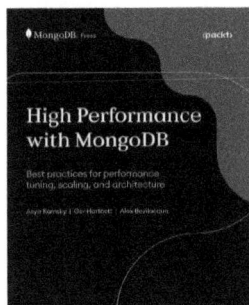

High Performance with MongoDB

Asya Kamsky, Ger Hartnett, Mr. Alex Bevilacqua

ISBN: 978-1-83702-263-2

- Diagnose and resolve common performance bottlenecks in deployments
- Design schemas and indexes that maximize throughput and efficiency
- Tune the WiredTiger storage engine and manage system resources for peak performance
- Leverage sharding and replication to scale and ensure uptime
- Monitor, debug, and maintain deployments proactively to prevent issues
- Improve application responsiveness through client driver configuration

## Packt is searching for authors like you

If you're interested in becoming an author for Packt, please visit authors.packt.com and apply today. We have worked with thousands of developers and tech professionals, just like you, to help them share their insight with the global tech community. You can make a general application, apply for a specific hot topic that we are recruiting an author for, or submit your own idea.

## Share your thoughts

Now that you've finished *MongoDB Essentials*, we'd love to hear your thoughts! Scan the QR code below to go straight to the Amazon review page for this book and share your feedback or leave a review on the site that you purchased it from.

https://packt.link/r/1806706091

Your review is important to us and the tech community, and will help us make sure we're delivering excellent quality content.

# Download a free PDF copy of this book

Thanks for purchasing this book!

Do you like to read on the go but are unable to carry your print books everywhere?

Is your eBook purchase not compatible with the device of your choice?

Don't worry, now with every Packt book you get a DRM-free PDF version of that book at no cost.

Read anywhere, any place, on any device. Search, copy, and paste code from your favorite technical books directly into your application.

The perks don't stop there, you can get exclusive access to discounts, newsletters, and great free content in your inbox daily.

Follow these simple steps to get the benefits:

1. Scan the QR code or visit the link below:

https://packt.link/free-ebook/9781806706099

2. Submit your proof of purchase.
3. That's it! We'll send your free PDF and other benefits to your email directly.

www.ingramcontent.com/pod-product-compliance
Ingram Content Group UK Ltd.
Pitfield, Milton Keynes, MK11 3LW, UK
UKHW061523250925
463267UK00001B/2

9 781806 706099